Contents

Where does meat come from? 4
What other food do we get
    from animals? 6
Where do cows live? 8
How big are farms? 10
Where do cows come from? 12
What happens when the calves
    are older? 14
What kind of meat do we
    get from cows? 16
What happens to the beef? 18
How does beef get to our table? 20
All kinds of food from animals! 22
Glossary 23
Find out more 24
Index 24

Where does meat come from?

Meat comes from animals. We get meat from lots of different animals. Meat can come from cows, sheep and chickens.

Meat contains **protein**. Protein is an important part of our diet. Our bodies need protein to stay healthy and strong.

What other food do we get from animals?

We also get **dairy** foods from animals. Dairy foods include milk, cheese and butter. Dairy foods also give us **protein**.

Another kind of animal that gives us food is fish. In this book we will look at how we get meat from cows.

Where do cows live?

Cows live on farms. They eat grass in fields. This is called grazing.

The farmer also feeds the cows hay in winter. The farmer looks after the cows. He makes sure they stay healthy.

How big are farms?

Some farms are large. They have big fields with many animals. They may have other kinds of animals as well as cows.

Other farms are small. They have a few
animals in a small field. The farmer gets
dairy foods from his animals as well
as meat.

Where do cows come from?

A baby cow is called a calf. Calves (more than one calf) are born on farms. Their mothers feed the calves milk.

When they are older, the calves start to eat grass like their mothers. The calves grow big and strong.

What happens when the calves are older?

When the calves are big enough, the farmer takes them to a market.

At the market, some of the calves are sold to other farmers. Other calves are sold to **butchers** for meat.

What kind of meat do we get from cows?

Meat from cows is called beef. **Butchers** cut the beef into joints, steaks and ribs.

Beef can be also be **minced**. Minced beef can be made into burgers.

What happens to the beef?

Butchers store the beef in large **refrigerators**. This keeps the beef fresh. All kinds of meat can also be frozen in freezers.

The beef is then packed into refrigerated lorries. The lorries take the beef to supermarkets and other shops. Beef is also sold in butchers' shops.

How does beef get to our table?

Shop workers put the beef into **refrigerators** in the shops. They put the same cuts of meat together.

We can choose the kind of beef we like to eat. The beef has come a long way from farm to fork!

All kinds of food from animals!

Different animal meats that we eat include beef, chicken, turkey and lamb.

Eggs are a good source of **protein**. Eggs come from chickens.

Salmon, trout and cod are all popular fish that we eat.

Glossary

butcher person who cuts up and sells meat

dairy relating to milk and the products made from it, such as butter and cheese

minced cut or chopped into very small pieces

protein substance found in meat, cheese, eggs and fish; our bodies need protein to keep healthy

refrigerator appliance for keeping our food cool

Find out more

Books

All About Meat and Fish (Food Zone), Victoria Parker
(QEB Publishing, 2010)
Food from Farms (World of Farming), Nancy Dickmann
(Raintree, 2010)

Websites

**https://learnenglishkids.britishcouncil.org/en/
category/topics/food**
This website contains lots of fun, food-based games for
you to play.

Index

beef 16, 17, 18, 19, 20, 21
butchers 15, 16, 18, 19
cows 4, 7, 8, 9, 10, 12, 16
dairy foods 6, 11
farms 8, 10, 11, 12, 21

meat 4, 5, 7, 11, 15, 16, 18, 20
protein 5, 6
shops 19, 20